For Gracelynn,
Watch out for they're
these guys —
dangerous!

Janet Piehocky

Poisons and Venom:

ANIMAL WEAPONS AND DEFENSES

BY JANET RIEHECKY

CONTENT CONSULTANT:
JACKIE GAI, DVM
ZOO AND EXOTIC ANIMAL VETERINARIAN

READING CONSULTANT:
BARBARA J. FOX
READING SPECIALIST
PROFESSOR EMERITUS
NORTH CAROLINA STATE UNIVERSITY

CAPSTONE PRESS
a capstone imprint

Blazers is published by Capstone Press,
1710 Roe Crest Drive, North Mankato, Minnesota 56003.
www.capstonepub.com

 Books published by Capstone Press are manufactured with paper containing at least 10 percent post-consumer waste.

Library of Congress Cataloging-in-Publication Data
Riehecky, Janet, 1953–
   Poisons and venom : animal weapons and defenses / by Janet Riehecky.
   p. cm. — (Blazers. Animal weapons and defenses)
   Includes bibliographical references and index.
   Summary: "Describes how animals use poison and venoms as weapons and defenses"—
Provided by publisher.
   ISBN 978-1-4296-6504-9 (library binding)
   ISBN 978-1-4296-8008-0 (paperback)
1. Poisonous animals—Juvenile literature. I. Title. II. Series.
QL100.R54 2012
591.6'5—dc23   2011034682

Editorial Credits

Mandy Robbins, editor; Kyle Grenz, designer; Svetlana Zhurkin, media researcher;
   Laura Manthe, production specialist

Photo Credits

Alamy: Carlos Villoch MagicSea, 8–9; Corbis: Kevin Schafer, 24–25; Dreamstime: Geoffrey
Kuchera, 15; iStockphoto: Mark Kostich, 22–23; Minden Pictures/Satoshi Kuribayashi, 16–17;
Newscom: WENN/ZOB/CB2, 20–21; Photolibrary: Christophe Véchot, 28–29; Shutterstock:
AlessandroZocc, 18–19, Audrey Snider-Bell, 26–27, Bruce MacQueen, 4–5, Cathy Keifer, 10–11,
John Arnold, 6–7, vblinov, cover (top), 12–13, worldswildlifewonders, cover (bottom)

Printed in the United States of America in
Stevens Point, Wisconsin.
102011   006404WZS12

TABLE OF CONTENTS

SMALL BUT DEADLY

Sometimes small creatures are the most deadly. They don't have to be big and strong. They have poison. Some animals use poison to defend themselves. Others use it to catch prey.

prey—an animal that is hunted by another animal for food

4

★ FIERCE FACT ★

The green lacewing is an insect that can spray an attacker with poison.

GREEN LACEWING

POISONOUS DEFENSES

The poison arrow frog is one of the deadliest animals in the world. Its skin is covered with slimy poison. Its bright colors warn **predators** not to touch it.

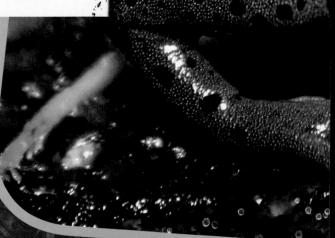

☆ FIERCE FACT ☆

A poison arrow frog has enough poison to kill 10 people.

predator—an animal that hunts other animals for food

Almost every part of a puffer fish's body is poisonous to predators. It even has poisonous spines. One puffer fish has enough poison to kill 30 people.

Poison isn't the puffer fish's only defense. When it is attacked, this fish puffs up to look bigger.

Monarch caterpillars eat poisonous milkweed. If an animal eats a monarch butterfly, it can get sick. It won't eat another orange butterfly again!

Eating 45 blister beetles could kill a 500-pound (227-kilogram) horse.

Blister beetles protect themselves with poisonous blood. If a beetle is attacked, it can make itself bleed. The blood gives attackers painful blisters.

TOXIC SPRAY

Skunks keep attackers away with a harmful, stinky spray. They release the spray from two sacs behind their tails. The **toxic** spray can cause temporary blindness.

★ FIERCE FACT ★

Skunks can spray targets as far as 10 feet (3 meters) away.

toxic—poisonous

The bombardier beetle mixes two chemicals in its abdomen to make a poison. The poison shoots out at a predator. The harmful spray is boiling hot.

abdomen—the rear part of an insect's body

A fire salamander has rows of poison **glands** behind its eyes and down its body. Its spray irritates the eyes and mouth of an attacker.

gland—a part of the body that produces a specific substance that is either used in the body or released by the body

A spitting cobra sprays venom from small holes in its fangs. The snake aims at the eyes of its attacker. The venom can cause blindness.

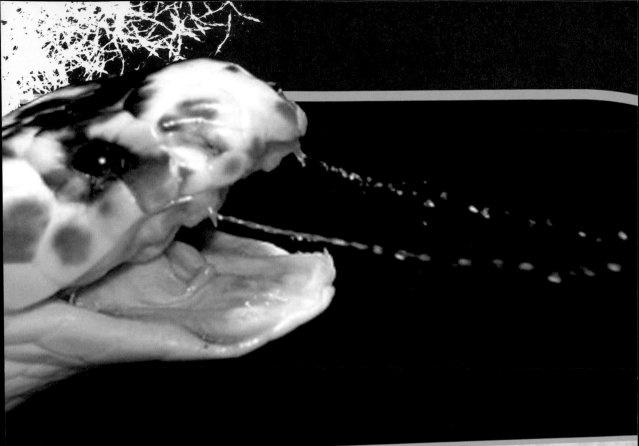

☆ *FIERCE FACT* ☆

The spitting cobra can hit the eyes of an attacker from 8 feet (2.4 m) away.

venom—poison inside the fangs of some animals

fang—a long, hollow tooth; venom flows through fangs

VENOMOUS BITES OR STINGS

Black widow spiders use their fangs to inject venom into prey. The venom turns the prey's insides to liquid. The black widow then slurps up the soupy mixture.

Killer bees are quicker to attack than ordinary honey bees. When threatened, large groups of killer bees attack at once. They use their stingers to inject venom. The multiple stings are painful and can be deadly.

☆ FIERCE FACT ☆

Killer bees may chase a person as far as 0.25 mile (0.4 km).

Rattlesnakes have sacs of poison in
their jaws. When they open their mouths to
strike, fangs spring forward. Venom flows
through the fangs and into prey.

A scorpion has two venom glands in its tail. When it strikes, the venom pours into a stinger at the end of the tail. The scorpion jabs the stinger into its prey.

Scorpions can survive on as little as one meal a year.

GLOSSARY

abdomen (AB-duh-muhn)—the rear part of an insect's body

fang (FANG)—a long, hollow tooth; venom flows through fangs

gland (GLAND)—a part of the body that produces a specific substance that is either used elsewhere in the body or is released by the body

predator (PRED-uh-tur)—an animal that hunts other animals for food

prey (PRAY)—an animal hunted by another animal for food

toxic (TOK-sik)—poisonous

venom (VEN-uhm)—a poisonous liquid that is injected into prey

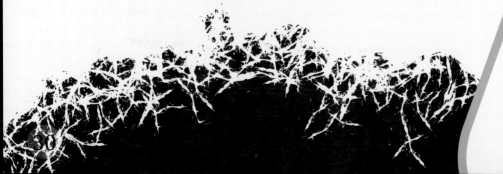

★ READ MORE ★

Dale, Jay. *Top Ten Snakes.* Deadly and Incredible Animals. Mankato, Minn.: Smart Apple Media, 2012.

Pryor, Kimberley Jane. *Venom, Poison, and Electricity.* Animal Attack and Defense. New York: Marshall Cavendish Benchmark, 2010.

Simon, Seymour. *Poisonous Animals.* Top 50 Questions. New York: Scholastic, 2007.

INTERNET SITES

FactHound offers a safe, fun way to find Internet sites related to this book. All of the sites on FactHound have been researched by our staff.

Here's all you do:

Visit *www.facthound.com*

Type in this code: 9781429665049

Super-cool stuff!   Check out projects, games and lots more at
www.capstonekids.com

INDEX